starlit
dreams.

ISBN: 9798859200788

by bella karad,
for you.

part of
starlit dreams.

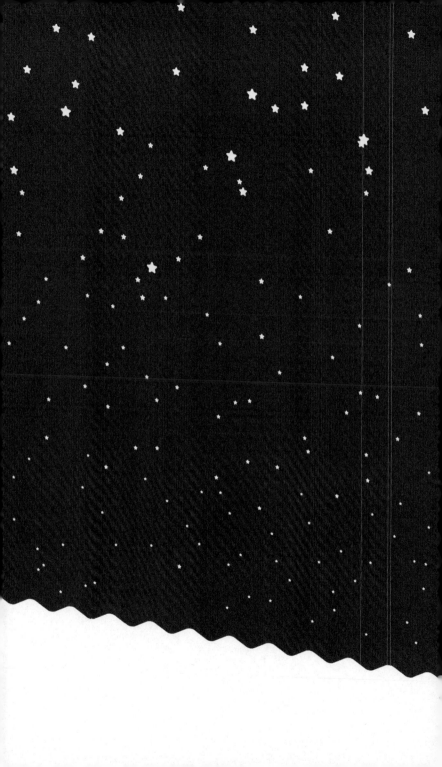

there's a part of me
that doesn't want to admit this,
but i am not crazy in love with you.

it doesn't feel like thundering storms,
or exploding fireworks, or burning flames.
my heart doesn't skip a beat
every time you look at me.

this love is peaceful and quiet,
it's gentle and calm.
it eases my mind;
it slows down my heartbeat;
and it allows me to heal.

it's not how i imagined love,
but it's the kind of love i needed.

i didn't fall in love with you at first glance.
my love for you grew slowly, with time.

it was the way you held my hand,
the way you looked at me
from across the room,
the way your eyes lit up
when you smiled at me,
the way your scent stayed
on my clothes for days;
the way you made me
feel safe in your presence.

i didn't fall in love with you at first glance.
i fell in love with the way you loved me.

no one has ever seen me
the way you do.

i've been called pretty before,
but no one has ever looked at me
like i was a pink sunset
or a starry night sky.

i'm sorry if i ever show signs of jealousy.
but the only reason for that
is that no one in my life
has ever made me feel
like nothing could ever
replace me.

it scares me to think about
just how much love i have for you,
and how i will never be able
to stop loving you.

because if you ever left,
i would be cursed to love you
until the end of time.

you are the kindest soul i've ever met.
you made me feel like i belong with you,
like i was meant to find you,
like we were destined to be.

never in my life did i think
that somewhere out there,
among billions of souls,
was a souls like yours.

i don't think i tell you this enough,
but i believe you were sent to me,
to be my safe place,
to be my home.

if i could,
i would hide you from the world.

your soul is too pure,
and your heart is too full of love,
to be faced with the cruelty
and ruthlessness of society.

i don't want this world
to change anything about you.

i thought i knew what love meant.
i tried so hard not to fall for you,
because i thought that to love
was just another way to get hurt.

but you taught me that love
doesn't have to be that way.
because loving you feels safe.
it feels fuzzy and warm.
it feels like home.

when i look at photos of you
or read your texts,
i wonder what i did
to deserve you.

it's hard to comprehend
that i found you
when i wasn't
even looking,
and that you stayed
when i wasn't
even expecting it.

when we were watching the stars
and you were looking up at them
i don't think you realized
that you were shining brighter
than every single one of them.

you are not just my favorite person.

you are also my favorite hug,
makes me feel safe and cared for.

you are my favorite voice,
so comforting and familiar.

you are my favorite smile,
genuine and so warm.

you are my favorite laughter,
infectious and bright.

you are my favorite feeling,
memory,
thought,
heart,
soul—

you are my favorite everything.
you are my everything.

the universe had a plan
and it was to give me a person
who my soul could belong to.

i don't tell you this enough,
but i'm so thankful for you.

thank you for coming into my life.
for making me smile.
for making me laugh.
for making me happy.

i'm thankful that the universe sent you,
and i'm thankful that you found me.

sometimes when i miss you
i just sit there and imagine
little scenarios of us in my head.

scenarios like getting coffee together, watching movies,
going for walks, cuddling in bed, having deep
conversations, going on late night food runs, taking
random trips, holding hands, sharing new music with
each other.

i just want to be with you.

even if i don't show it,
i hope you know
how much i appreciate it
when you talk to me.
because sometimes i feel
too isolated and unloved
to come to you first.

i'll keep you safe
in my arms;
just hold on
and you'll see.

since i've been yours,
each day seems to have
plenty more sunshine
for lovely things to do
with you.

i got addicted to you so easily.
and attracted to you in ways
i can't even explain.

i care about you
more than you think.
i think about you
more than you realize.
i appreciate you
more than you will ever know.
you're the first and the last thing
on my mind each and every day.

no words are good enough
to describe exactly how
you make me feel.

i may not be the first woman in your life, but i want to be the last. i know i'm not the one who first made you feel loved, but i want to be the only one to make you feel loved to the core. i promise to treat you the way you want to be treated, and give you the respect you deserve. i promise to always be your lover and your friend. i will always pay attention and give you time. i promise to always share what's in my heart and on my mind. i just want to say that i love you, will always love you, and that you are the only person i'll ever love this much.

i didn't fall in love with you
because i was looking for someone.
i didn't fall in love with you
because i felt too alone on my own.
i didn't fall in love with you
because i needed a relationship
to be happy.

i fell in love with you
because you make me feel needed.
i fell in love with you
because when i give you my love,
you give me yours in return.
i fell in love with you
because you radiate
a very special energy.

i fell in love with you
because you are you.

we could sit in silence for hours;
that's what i love about you the most—
the comfortable silence.

you know, i adore you more than you could ever imagine. it is you who enters my mind every time i wake up and every time i go to sleep. it is you who i think of when i look at the sunrise, the sunset, the moon, the flowers, the ocean, and everything that is beautiful. it is you who i see when i think of the future. the one i sit with on the porch, the one i sleep with, the person who i go home to after a long day at work. you are the person i imagine spending my life with. you are my comfort, and my home, and my best friend. my lover, my person, my future. you are the only person who holds my heart. the one who i dedicate all my poems to. and if love was a person, it would be you.

i was never good at showing my emotions.

i'm shy, and i'm too scared
to go outside of my comfort zone.

sometimes it's hard for me
to express my emotions
let alone express my love;
but i love you.

so i may not be able to say it
or to act like it;
i may show less effort than most,
but you can always count on me
for one thing:

i will never fail to show my love through writing.
you are worth more than a million poems,
so i'll write a million poems
for you.

everything has changed
ever since i met you;
the breeze blows warmer,
the flowers smell nicer,
the moon shines brighter,
the stars seem more numerous;
suddenly, sunsets became more beautiful,
and i want to watch every single one with you.

my hands are yours to hold onto
and my shoulders are yours to cry on.
lay down on my chest, my love,
and let me absorb some of your burden.

i promise i will never leave.

i was never really a fan of love.
then you happened.

i didn't really want it at first,
but your love pushed through to me.
i fell in love with the way
you made the morning sun
shine a little warmer,
and the midnight moon
shine a little brighter.
i fell in love with the way i smile
to every message you send me;
from your sweet good mornings
to your lovely good nights.

i fell in love the way you made me feel.
i fell in love with you.

there's no better match
than me and you.
now that i've found you,
i'm never letting go.

i wish i had the guts
to ask you to grow old with me,
but until i can utter these words
i'll just say *i love you* at every sunrise.

i was always told to take risks.
well,
i listened,
and i can now say that
you are the greatest risk i've ever taken,
and the greatest reward.

i'm here for the days
when you need someone to talk to,
and here for the days
when you feel like the world is against you.

you deserve
to be loved
without feeling
that you have to hide
the parts of you
that you think
are unlovable.

years from today
i want to see myself
loving the same person
i love right now.

let's grow together.

if the stars could write,
i hope that in every lifetime
they write your name
on the same page as mine.

starlit dreams — bella karad

in your next lifetime
pay attention to the wind;
i will keep saying your name
and hope that the wind
leads you back to me.

time spent with you
never feels wasted.

we could sit
in silence
for hours
and it would feel like
just a moment
in time.

maybe this
sounds stupid
but sometimes
when i go to bed
i hug my pillow
and pretend
that it's you.

i don't think i'll ever know how to love someone else the way i love you. you are the last person i ever want to love like this, and i promise you that i will hold onto us until my last breath escapes me.

you will always be
the one my soul searches for
in every lifetime.

i love you
because i never
had to tell you
who i was.

you already knew.

when i met you
it felt like your soul
reached out to mine
took its hand
and promised
to keep it safe forever.

the way you make me feel
is how i want to feel
until the day after forever.

i need you to know
that i won't let go
not now, not ever.

it has always been
and it will always be
you and me.

at the other side of this life,
whatever that may be,
i hope that it is with you.

my love for you will last
even if the lover leaves.

you are not hard to love. loving you is the easiest thing i have ever done. feels as if i was made to do it. my heart is so full of unconditional love for you. when i look at you, all i can feel is pure love. it's not hard to love you. it's impossible not to.

one day
we will wake up
in the same bed,
but in our 70s,
and i pray we have
matching smile wrinkles
beneath our eyes.

and i promise you
that whenever i look
at the moon
the sun rays
the sunsets
the mountains
the seas
the flowers
i will always remember
that our love is as beautiful
as the most beautiful things in life.

if life
were a book
then meeting you
was my favorite chapter.

~and i will forever remember your page number.

finally,
i found my happiness,

and it's you.

they asked me:
are you in love?

and suddenly,
my cheeks felt warm and pink,
butterflies filled my stomach,
and i caught myself smiling.

i am.

when my cheeks kept hurting from smiling,
my heart kept fluttering,
my legs felt weak,
and eye contact with you became my favorite thing,
that's when i realized:

the longer i stare at you
the more beautiful you become;
silky hair, sparkling eyes,
soothing voice, soft lips,
kindest heart

you're mesmerizing.

and to the universe
i have only one thing to say;

thank you for making this person mine.

if you ever need to lay down on my chest
and cover it in tears
i will gladly let you, hold you,
until you fall asleep.

i want your happiest moments to be with me,
but i am your home for dark things, too.

it's weird how
we could spend
a whole day together
and i would still miss you
the second you leave.

the way you look at me,
the way you hold my hand,
the way you kiss my cheek,
the way you hug me tightly,
the way you smile at me,
the way you cuddle me all night,
the way you talk about me,
the way you talk about *us*.

i love being loved by you.

the more you unravel yourself to me,
the more deeply i feel for you.

you are more than enough to me
and if you can't accept that yet,
i hope that one day you will.

i don't want to lose you,
because that would mean
i've lost my own heart.

you will either be the one i marry,
or my worst heartbreak.

you're the first person who has truly made me feel safe and loved. you make me happy, you make me laugh and you make me smile. you're the most gorgeous, amazing, funniest, caring, loving, sweetest person in the entire universe. it's like i can talk to you for hours, even days, and you would never get bored; you would actually listen. i can talk to you about anything, and you would never judge me. i get so happy when i wake up to see your notification on my phone. i think about you day and night; you're always on my mind, no matter what i'm doing. i love it when i get to hear your voice and your laugh. i know i could be a little annoying or a mess, but you're still here for me, and i thank you so much for that. i don't know how i got so lucky, but i did, and this relationship is something that i could never regret. i love you so much, and i think you should know that.

meeting you
was one of the
best moments
of my life.

at the end of the day,
you're the person
i want to come home to.

you're the person
i want to tell about my day.

you're the person
i want to share
my happiness,
sadness,
frustration,
and success with.

and i will spend every day
for the rest of my life
proving this to you.

you healed pieces of me
i didn't know needed healing.

you cared for me when
i didn't know i could use
that extra love.

you brought out
the happiness in me
i didn't know existed.

you've made me feel
more alive than ever.

be mine forever.

i fell in love with you
not knowing what love really was.
i stayed in love with you
because there's no one
i've ever wanted more than you.
i will forever be in love with you
because i can't picture even
a second of my life without you.

i'm so grateful for you every second. i'm grateful that we met. i'm grateful that somehow, in this crazy universe with infinite possibilities, destiny paved the way for us to see each other at the right time, in the right place, at the right moment. so many things could have happened to keep us from existing together. yet we met and started something so beautiful. i'm grateful for us, and i never want to let you go.

i only want two things in this world:
i want you and i want us.

to you:

i love you.
and i will do everything i can to make us work. because
i want a future with you, to spend my life with you, to
grow old with you. because you are the only person i
want to be with. so, will you step on the boat and sail in
the sea in this adventure with me?

from the moment you walked into my life, you became a cherished chapter in my story. a chapter filled with love, laughter, and countless beautiful moments. you are more than just a partner to me. you're my best friend. your presence in my life has brought a kind of happiness that i never thought possible. your love has touched my heart in the most profound way, and i am endlessly grateful for the love we share. in your arms, i find comfort and safety. your laughter is music to my ears, and your smile brightens even the gloomiest of days. your love has a way of making everything feel right, of making every challenge seem conquerable, and of turning ordinary moments into treasured memories. with you, i've experienced a love that is pure, genuine, and truly extraordinary. your support, your kindness, and your understanding have shown me what it means to be loved unconditionally. you've brought out the best in me and i am a better person because of your love. as we continue our journey through life together, i want you to know that my love for you grows stronger with each passing day. i cherish every moment we spend together, and i look forward to the countless adventures that await us. i want to express my heartfelt gratitude for your love, your companionship, and the joy you bring into my life. thank you for being the incredible person that you are, for sharing your heart with me, and for allowing me to be a part of your world. no matter where life's path takes us, please know that my love for you is unwavering. you are my dearest love, and i feel blessed to have you.

your heart is so full of gold
i believe you might be an angel.

if you were the rain
i would never open an umbrella.
i would lay down on the cold concrete
and enjoy every drop that lands on my skin.
i would lay there even if it meant i could drown in you.

when people are in love, they often say they simply fell, tripped over their own two feet, face forward, and into the arms of their beloved. i did more than simply fall onto the ground of your love. you, for me, were an ocean, and i dived headfirst, roughly, harshly, almost painfully into the waters of *you*. i knew i could not swim, but i did so anyway. i was drowning, entangled in you, surrounded by this being of *you*, engulfed in this feeling of *you*. and i didn't know what came over me, but i let myself drown. i did not try to swim back up because if i went back to land, releasing myself from your grasp, that would mean losing the feeling of *you*. and after submerging into the depth, the love, the passion of *you*, how could i ever leave?

you asked me why i like you
but i didn't want to tell
some of my reasons are cheesy...
but here is why i fell

i love the way your lips curve
when i make you smile
it makes me want to pull you close
and kiss you for awhile

i love the way your eyes twinkle
when you talk about things you love
i truly believe
you are a gift from above

i love that you are compassionate
you have such a big heart
that was the first thing i noticed
right from the start

i love the way it feels
when you hold me tight
i finally feel safe
like i could sleep through the night

i love that you don't judge me
for my less than perfect self
that is more attractive
than any amount of wealth

there are so many more reasons
but i'll start with these few
maybe someday
i'll give this poem to you

as i lie here with eyes closed softly, i think deeply of you, and i inhale stars — the scent of twinkling light, so fresh and alive, sparkling gently inside me. and i want to write this feeling so tentatively, as it must be, like writing words on bubbles, delicate and precious, begging them not to disappear like dreams in the morning.

our love proved
that magic is real.

we were timeless
built to last lifetimes

when the night ends
i think about beginning it
only with you

the ocean was my deepest escape
so i swam until i found you

i saw a glimpse
of what our
heaven could be.

we were lost under a purple sunset
and for the first time in forever
i didn't want to be found.

the way your smile can light the darkest room,
or shelter me from the worst storm
was something to behold,
you could make my off days so much better
with so little effort,
it's almost unbearable.

the way your kiss, softer than a cloud,
sweeter than the nectar of the gods,
can make honey bees blush,
i could live forever in that moment,
i long to feel the rush.

if my fate is to love you
then i'll burn for you
like a star in your night sky
bright, steady, reliable
unwavering
until the end of time.

let's take pictures
not together
but of each other
so when you look at the picture
you remember the moment
not because you see me there
but because you relive the moment
all over again.

starlit dreams — bella karad

i carved your name upon the dawn
so every morning might be with you
but as it rose it grew too bright
and closed my eyes
yet i still saw you there

i carved your name upon the sky
to keep you near me every day
but nightfall came and cleared the light
and all was dark
yet i still saw you there

i carved your name upon the moon
to stare at you throughout my nights
but tired eyes are sneaky foes
and sleep prevailed
yet i still saw you there

i carved your name upon my soul
so that every day and every night
and in my heart
i still see you there

on this night let's take a walk
together just you and me,
holding hands we'll count stars
with a kiss for each, we see.

loving you is like breathing,
true beauty of a heavenly design,
just as our seeds of love were sown,
forever into a growing vine.

as angels sing of beautiful love,
filling the sweet-scented night air,
a joyful melody of sound,
reveals the love we share.

on this night let's take a walk
until the sun meets our star-filled eyes,
and then when the stars twinkle and shine
we'll walk again through paradise.

i never knew
about
true love
until
the day
you
touched
my
heart.

what does it feel like to be held
not by another body
not by a set of limbs, a chest, a chin
but by another soul?

what does it feel like
to see truth in another pair of eyes
instead of hidden intentions
instead of absence?

what does it feel like
to hear a familiar heartbeat
resounding next to your own
reaching through skin
through bone
two rhythms
indistinguishable?

because of you,
all of this is answered.

i want to swim
in a ocean
that tastes
like you.

your soft touch
warms my heart
you fill my life with
happiness and joy
and the way you slowly
kiss me,
one glance at you
and i'm in love
when you walk by
people stare at you, you're beautiful
you're an angel from above
you're the one i truly love
you fill my heart with
complete desire
your soft touch
warms my heart
and sets my
soul on fire.

we sat there in silence,
side by side,
hand in hand,
letting the crimson sunset
pour out its last waves of light.
tonight is about us, my love,
nothing else is real—
let time stand still.

if i were a poem
i'd be made of words
that only you'd understand.

your soul
is a bookmark
just open
to the page
forever
true love
no matter
our age.

you.
are.
a.
walking.
masterpiece.

when you kissed me goodnight
i held on with tears in my eyes
and usually i don't hold onto anyone.

i wanted a star
but you gave me
the galaxies of your heart.

nestled in your arms, i've discovered a haven,
the refuge for my soul, a home is engraven.
a sanctuary where thoughts find gentle release,
a world of unity, my doubts meet their peace.

when weariness tugs and desolation entwines,
life's enigmatic encounters, weaving complex designs,
in your gaze serenity blooms and finds its place,
a sanctuary of solace, a loving embrace.

within your eyes, a realm beyond time,
where enchantment flows in a fractal rhyme.
familiar, like an ancient whisper, this truth so pure,
innocence cascades, beauty's allure.

through you a passage to celestial expanse,
an orchestra of emotions, our souls entwine and dance.
each moment evolves, exquisitely hued,
at the threshold of forever, together with you.

life's intricate threads lead to a destined connection,
guiding me to you, the most profound intersection.
gratitude rises, an endless ocean's plea,
for destiny's masterpiece, in you, i see.

baby, there's no need to go outside.
let the rain keep you in my arms tonight.
baby, please, can't you see
just how happy you make me?

hold me in your arms tight.
let me dance around you
grab a few drinks with me, darling.
take a walk in the moonlight,
going down to the ocean.

let's go enjoy the sights in the dead of night,
feel the sand beneath our feet,
hear the ocean around us.

let me take your hand
while we start dancing in the sand,
the sea breeze cooling our flushed cheeks,
the moon reflecting in our eyes
as we enjoy the night,
finding peace in each other's company.

i think we were destined from the first time
i heard you speak,
a rough but gentle voice you carry,
and i hope you know it carries me.

i feel i've known you for ages,
even though it's only been a short while.
sometimes, i wish i could meet you all over again.

you're a rush of air,
something i've needed for so long.
sometimes, it's so hard to breathe around here.

in such a way that seems elementary,
i want to write the loveliest things about you.
i want to put them in the sky.

but in the same way,
i want nobody to know.
i want to go with you wherever you slip away to.

and i want you to slip away to me.
i want to be that embrace
that lets you know you're home
because you let me know the same.

loving you is the smell of the rain
fresh. life-sustaining.
sweet droplets dripping on petals
blooming in spring.

loving you is breath catching in my chest
overwhelmed and afraid
because it's so good I fret
the concept of ever having to spend
a day of this life without you in it.

loving you is the depth of
the sea
so vast that even its
contemplation is greater than is
humanly conceivable,
the feeling of warm saltwater on
tanned skin,
sounds of
crashing waves,
loving you is a perfect summer day.

loving you is a rocket to outer space
lost in the cosmos
i'm living amongst the constellations
draped against
the milky way;
loving you,
being loved by you,
looms larger than this world.

loving you is the most
beautiful terrifying expansive
life-altering mind-blowing unimaginable
gift

that i never would've dreamed of finding
let alone deserving.

loving you is absolute magic;
because you are absolutely magical."

you hold a different, yet familiar beauty
free of thought but full of intention
melody and harmony dance to your voice
powerful tenderness held in your eyes,
with gentle strength in your hands
all leaving me silent, in awe.

there's comfort and calm,
in your house, in you—
like a different realm,
after all we've been through.

your small touch— gaze alone—
is a home. do you know?

your lips taste
of frosted starlight
crystal eyes fixed on mine
you could wish upon
a falling star
and i'd never stop
loving you.

when you become old,
grey and withered;
i'd still display you in a vase.

i never believed in happy endings
because they never really seemed to exist
not until i met you
not until you made me believe, and i couldn't resist

resist you and me. we were so impossible
never did i know, i'd love you with all my heart
and you'd love me too, for who i am
but now that we do, i can delightedly say that you are
my life and not just a part.

i want to wake up
fifty years
from now
when time will
be right

but for tonight
let me close my eyes
and put my head
on your chest
to rest for a second

for a little moment
that only could
be us.

i once dreamed of love,
a love that is so pure,
a love that is so kind.

the day i bumped into a single road,
was the day i bumped into love i never expected.

love has never crossed my mind,
not ever.
but love comes unexpectedly,
at times when i least expected it.

but love is so kind,
love is so pure,
love strengthens my wings,
love leads a journey to an infinite galaxy.

and love is no longer a dream.

you remind me of someone
i've met a long time ago.
i can't put my finger on it,
but the longer i sit
and look into your eyes,
the present day dies,
and i am taken back
to a distant past,
divided by love and war.
i swear, on my dead corpse,
we were together.
maybe we're meant for each other
until the end of time?

love is like a white pearl
at the bottom of the sea
it's hard to find, but you believe
in its immortal promise...

your other half is out there
waiting for you.

you make me feel beautiful
in three ways;

one - by calling me beautiful,
two - by looking at me with such
loving eyes,
and most importantly,
three - by being with you.

thank you for
looking at me
with such kindness
in your eyes,
love in your veins,
and warmth in
the wrinkles
surrounding
your eyelashes.

i don't think anyone loves the way i do,
i don't think anyone can love
the way i love you.

i know they don't, and no matter what you do,
i won't stop loving you,

the way just i do.

i'll never regret
choosing you
to make
my heart
smile

i love you so much
more than the sun loves the moon,
or the day loves the noon.
i want to hug you more than
waves hug the shore,
or a frame hugs a door,
and kiss you more than the
horizon does the sky
or more than lashes bat an eye.
i don't think i could love you more,
but now, i've said that before,
and i'll say it over and over
until the day i die.

i want to be your other half
so good at loving you
not even sunshine could warm you up
make you glow like i do.

loving a ghost boy,
brown, gentle eyes,
dark flowing hair,
you magnetize me,
love soft as the sky,
enigmatic, beautiful,
out of a shadowy night
your love finds me,
and i find you,
ghost boy,
boy that i love.

you're my first.

and i don't mean my first kiss,
or my first relationship,
or my first *i love you.*

you're the first person
who makes me feel like i'm enough
and the first one to show me
what *i love you* actually means.

thank you for reading,
i love you.

part of
starlit
dreams.

discover the whole series:
mybook.to/StarlitDreamsTheSeries

starlit
dreams.

Printed in Great Britain
by Amazon